The Invisible
In
Plain Sight

By Robert Stowe

D1468977

Dedicated to

RandaLynn

The Invisible in Plain Sight

As a writer, I'm compelled to tell a story. My imagination is unleashed. Words appear on the paper then sentences and paragraphs inventing characters and situations. I create stories, plays, and poems. The world of fictional writing is at my command, but I want to experience something new. I don't want to create a story from my imagination; I want to tell one by discovering something that exists in the real world. I have only ventured into the world of nonfiction writing in poetry because the truth of my life hurts. I am not ready to expose those wounds by ripping off the protective scabs covering them. I've decided to live within a world that is invisible but in plain sight. I will tell the truth of those who are feared and detested. I will tell their unheard stories.

The moisture in my nostrils freezes instantly as I step out of Ogilvie station into the frigid January morning in the Windy City. I decide to walk to my destination on Michigan Avenue rather than take a cab. I don't want to draw undue attention to myself. I have left all of my worldly possessions at home. I am dressed in many layers of clothing I purchased from a second-hand store just down the block from my house. My face is covered in a week's worth of stubble. I only carry with me a used backpack filled with a few more articles of clothing, a pillow, and a cardboard sign. I have a sleeping bag tied to the top of the backpack for easy transport. These will be my only possessions for the next month.

I head towards Michigan Avenue because I know where to find the community I'm looking for. They populate different areas of the sidewalks and corners along this main drag of Chicago's loop. I find a place amongst the crowd, claiming my territory in front of Dylan's Candy Bar. I pull out my cardboard sign that reads "Homeless Veteran Please Help." The large

Dunkin Donuts coffee I got at the train station has been consumed and now becomes my depository. I sit down and pretend to look miserable; it doesn't take long sitting in the cold to actually become miserable.

After hours of sitting on the cold concrete I'm unable to handle it anymore. I need to stretch my cramped muscles and find something warm to drink to help dispel the cold that has penetrated my bones. Food isn't a necessity at this time because I want to experience what it's like to go hungry for a day. I am shooed from a few stores for my appearance before I find a place that will serve me a cup of coffee without judging me for who they think I am. I sip my coffee. I'm trying to think of what the next step in my adventure will be. I need to find a place to sleep tonight, but I have no idea where to find the homeless "camps." After all, the world of the homeless is invisible to the rest of us.

My coffee is gone, and I'm finally warm. The sun has been down for a while now. I must find a place to sleep before it gets too dark. I head out towards Millennium Park to hopefully find others who call the streets of Chicago home. I approach a group of about five individuals hoping they might be able to help.

"Hi. I'm looking for a place to sleep tonight."

The look of caution on the faces of four of the five individuals makes me take a step back, and I quickly explain.

"I'm new to Chicago, and I have no idea where to go. I've been chased off by several police officers already, and I don't want to be a bother."

"I am Elijah. You can follow us in a few minutes, and you can stay with us. We're just waiting for a few others.

"I am Craig Mueller," I say quickly, caught off guard, constructing the alias from names of people I grew up with. "It's nice to meet you, and thanks for helping me."

A half hour goes by easily with idle chit-chat before we head towards our destination. About twelve others have joined our group, and all of them are questioning who I am. Elijah tells them that I'm new to the area, and I remain quiet. After what seems like a military hike with full gear on, we arrive at our destination. It's a neighborhood under a highway. Not your typical neighborhood, but one made up of cardboard homes, oil drum fire pits, and roofs constructed of old sheets and blankets. I have to hold back tears after seeing this. How is it that people can survive like this when the rest of society has riches beyond their needs?

Elijah shows me a place I can claim as my own. It's nothing more than an old box laid out flat to keep me off of the dirt and rocks. I put my pack down and lay out my sleeping bag. I pull my pillow out of the backpack and put it with my sleeping bag. The bitter cold is starting to get to me again, and I need to be by the fire to keep warm. When I get to the fire I am introduced to the group. (I don't remember every name because so many came and went during my month-long stay. Those I do remember are the ones I talked to and befriended.)

"Once again, I'm Elijah. This is Bill, Harvey, Eric, and Victor. Over there you have Marissa and her children April and Ryle. The gentleman over there is who we call Crazy Henry. If you stay around long enough, you'll know why we call him that. I do caution that you stay away from him though because he might confuse you with someone in one of his flashbacks."

"I'm Craig Mueller. I'm not from around here. I appreciate you helping me out."

"Do you have any food for tonight? If not, we'll share, but you'll have to add to the pot tomorrow."

"No, sorry I don't have any food. I only made enough today to get coffee."

"Well, if you make more than $20 a day this time of the year, you're doing really good."

A few cans of beans are passed around, and the same spoon is used by everybody who eats from each can. A few loaves of bread are also passed around. A bottle of cheap whiskey is offered to me, but I refused it since I don't drink – not anymore. Thankfully I was prepared enough to fill my coffee cup with water before I left the coffee shop earlier, but water does not take off the chill of a wintry night as good as whiskey does.

I haven't been officially told, but I've come to realize that Elijah is the leader of this particular clan of individuals. He seems to speak for the group and take charge of situations that may arise. He tells us that it's getting late, and he suggests we settle in for the night. I head to my little place of heaven and kick off my shoes. I hunker down into my sleeping bag and zip myself up tight. I pull the string of my hoodie tight around my head and face so that my head is covered and protected. I lie down and try to sleep. The freezing air is too much to handle, and I begin to shiver.

"Do you have enough newspaper?" asks Bill, the man next to me.

"I can't read in the dark."

"It's not for reading. You crumple it up and put it inside of your clothes for insulation."

"Oh, that's a great idea. Thank you."

Bill hands me a stack of papers and one by one I crumple them up and put them inside of my shirt. The paper feels scratchy against my skin for the first few minutes, but once it's flattened enough by the weight of me it's no longer a bother. I close my eyes once again trying to fall asleep, but I'm haunted by the labored breathing of another individual near me. I can hear an insistent knocking in his chest with every breath he expels. I have only heard this knocking one other time in my life. I know it's the knock of death. I drift off to sleep dreaming of that feared hooded figure covered in black coming for me.

As I open my eyes the next morning my fears are confirmed. Death has paid us a visit. Elijah is standing over the man who has been taken to the place of no return. I don't remember the man's name, and I can't remember seeing him as we talked around the oil drum. I hold back tears because I don't feel letting my emotions get out of check is the right thing to do at this moment, but inside my heart a waterfall of tears crashes for this man.

The coroner leaves with the man who has expired. The group separates to go about their daily activities. I skip breakfast for a large cup of coffee and head back to my turf in front of Dylan's Candy Bar. It's another frigid day and a light dry snow is falling. My muscles are still stiff from yesterday and from sleeping on the ground. The pain is making it difficult for me to keep seated. I have to stretch several times throughout the day. At one point I take my extra blanket from my backpack and use it like a shawl to keep warm.

After rush hour subsides, I collect my belongings and head to a small grocery store to buy food to share with the group with my proceeds from the day. I have skipped both breakfast and lunch today, not because I wasn't hungry but because I want to know what it's like to go without food. If I'm going to learn from this excursion, I have to sacrifice a few things. Most people take for granted the things they own and the things they get to do. I do not have a home. I do not have a bathroom I can call my own. I do not get to shower every day. I have nowhere to wash my body or clothes on a daily basis. I can't even brush my teeth.

I decide to buy food that isn't very expensive. I want to make sure I provide enough for myself and everyone who wants to share. I select a package of rolls from the day-old rack, a few cans of beans, and two cans of Spam. I've never eaten Spam before, so this will be an adventure of its own. Once I pay for my purchase, I head to Millennium Park to join my companions for our walk back to our "neighborhood."

It's a quiet walk tonight. I'm not sure if it's the weather or the thought of that fellow companion no longer with us. Only a few people gather around the fire tonight. The air is heavy, as if Death had never left. Nobody shares any food, and only a few actually eat. I put the rest of what I bought in my backpack for tomorrow after only eating one roll myself. I head to my bed and stuff myself with newspaper once again. I zip myself into my sleeping bag, and I fall asleep rather quickly.

I'm jolted awake by a boot in my side. Elijah towers above me.

"Just making sure you're still alive kid. You slept past all the excitement."

"Excitement? What did I miss?"

"Couple of outsiders tried to make off with a few things that didn't belong to them. A small fight broke out, but nobody got hurt and nothing was taken."

"Wow, I must've slept hard. Where is everybody?"

"They've all left for the day. It's past 10 O'clock already."

"You're going out?"

"Not today. Today I look after Henry. I go out for two days and spend two days with Henry. That's my job. I don't need much to survive, but Henry needs me so he can live to see another day."

"I think I might sit in for the day as well. I made good money yesterday, and I don't think I want to face the world today."

"In that case pull up a milk crate and make yourself comfortable."

I seat myself on an old Dairy Farms milk crate next to Henry and across from Elijah. The nearby fire is keeping us warm. The freeway above us is keeping the downpour of snow off of us. A light wind breezes past us every now and then. The world around us moves along, but the two of us sit upon our milk crates chatting and becoming friends as we tend to the needs of another friend. Today is a good day.

Elijah

Elijah is a man of many adventures. He has had his wonderful moments and his hardships. Elijah is not living within the world of the homeless because he is trapped here. He is living this life by choice. Elijah was born in a small town in Alabama. He lived there with his family until he graduated high school. His parents were very proud of him. He was the first person in his family to have accomplished this.

A week after he graduated, he answered his call of duty and registered with the draft board and was then shipped off to basic training. The Vietnam Conflict was at its peak, and when he finished his training, he was sent to the front lines to defend the interests of the United States. It was in his second tour that he met Henry. Henry was a Lieutenant and took over Elijah's platoon after the previous Lieutenant was killed in action. Henry was not like any of the other soldiers. He seemed to care about everybody in his unit. Elijah believed it was because he hadn't been hardened by the war yet. Henry had only been in Vietnam for 11 days.

A month into Henry's tour the platoon was on patrol deep in the jungles of Vietnam. They came under fire and were surrounded by the enemy. Elijah was on the M-60 with another soldier, Gibson, who was feeding the rounds into the gun. They came under heavy fire and Gibson was hit and killed instantly. Elijah didn't see that he was in the crosshairs of the enemy's weapon when Henry jumped and shoved him to the ground. Henry took a bullet to the chest, and Elijah escaped unharmed. After an airstrike annihilated the enemy, Henry was rushed to the hospital for his wounds. That bullet had apparently come close to his heart. He was shipped back to the states after he healed. Elijah was sent home a week later. Elijah felt indebted to Henry for saving his life and promised to always be there for him no matter what.

After Elijah got home from the war and made his promise to Henry he decided to settle down. He found a good job working at a warehouse loading semi-trailers. He saved up for a few years and bought a house. This is something else his family never had the opportunity to do. His parents had rented the small apartment he was born and raised in. They lived out their days in that very same apartment. Elijah never felt the need to marry or have children, but he lived with and dated the same woman for fifteen years. When she passed away from cancer, he never felt the need to find another woman to spend his life with because he already had given his heart to her Nobody else could ever earn that honor from him again. How he ended up here is a story for another time.

Snow

After a long day of relaxing by the fire as the snow covered the world with its white blanket it's time to settle in. The rest of the clan returns early in the day because the snow has made it very difficult to make any money. The food I bought last night is shared amongst all of us. Despite the bitter cold we cheerfully eat and drink filling the night with song and stories. As the night comes to a close, I settle into my sleeping bag and happily dream the night away. All of my worries are forgotten. I feel peace within myself.

I awaken to find myself covered in the deceptively fluffy, bitterly cold snow. Three feet have fallen while we slept. Thankfully the wetness of the heavy snow hasn't penetrated the outside lining of my sleeping bag. I can't imagine sleeping in a frozen sleeping bag under a highway on the wintery streets of Chicago. Although the snow is deep and the air is frigid, I head back to my claim on the sidewalk in front of the candy store to try and collect a few dollars for the day.

Shortly after midday the snow begins to fall again, and it's heavier than the snow that fell through the night. I decide to call it quits and get something warm to drink. After a short trip to a convenience store for coffee and the grocery store for food I head back to my palace under the highway. I find a few boxes by the dumpster at the grocery store, and I build myself a makeshift house to cover my head during the night. Although we are all covered by the highway, the snow sometimes finds its way into our neighborhood via the wind and blankets us with its presence. Although I don't have enough cardboard to fully enclose myself from the elements, I am able to build a wall and roof to block the wind from reaching me.

The rest of the day sucks. A gale force wind is blowing in from the west and drives the snow in at a blinding pace. There is little anybody can do. We all huddle around the oil drums adding fuel periodically to keep the fire from going out. It's a difficult task in such a strong winter storm, but we manage to keep the fire going. It's around five-thirty that I notice April and Ryle, both age six, trying to arouse their mother to no avail. I take it upon myself to see if they need help. As I arrive to the scene, I notice the paleness of Marissa's skin. I immediately know she is not well. I call over to Bill, and he runs to my side. He quickly assesses the situation and runs for help. The rest of the group gathers around me as I try to keep the children calm. Marissa is still alive, but she is dreadfully ill. A few minutes have passed, and Bill returns. He says he has called the paramedics. He suggests that we hide the children so that the paramedics don't report them to the Department of Children and Families. He also suggests that someone go to the hospital with Marissa and look after her. I volunteer for this assignment.

The hospital air is stale and stagnant. It's pungent with antiseptic and disinfectant. The cold lime green of the walls placed atop the light gray tile of the floor in the room in which I wait is not comforting in the least. The family members of other patients quietly thumb through magazines and play on their smart phones reading the latest Facebook updates of their friends. Most of them look worried, but a few seem content only to interact with their phones. I don't know why I'm nervous, but anxiety has found me and is creeping its way into my thoughts. I have barely spoken to Marissa in the few days that I have spent on the streets of Chicago, but I'm worried for her. What will happen to her children if she is to become completely incapacitated or even die? Who will step up and take responsibility for April and Ryle? Will they continue to live on the streets or will they have to go to foster care? What about family members?

I haven't noticed, but the questions swimming through my head have tortured me in my sleep. I doze off, and the night passes me by. It's somewhere around three in the morning when I walk to the nurses' station and question the wellbeing of Marissa. The nurse asks if I'm a family member, and I tell her that I am Marissa's half-brother on our mother's side. The nurse looks at me suspiciously until she finds my name on the list of allowed visitors as Marissa's brother. I didn't know, but Marissa invented me as her brother when she was admitted to the hospital. She has been in and out of consciousness throughout the night, but she has managed to remember that I had ridden in the ambulance with her to the hospital.

The nurse tells me that Marissa has been taken to the third floor. Visiting hours are over, but since I have been there all night I can go up to the room and sit with her. When I step out of the elevator into the dimly light hallway, I notice the nurse coming out of Marissa's room. As she walks away from me, I slip into the room. Marissa is sitting up in her bed with her eyes closed. It appears that she is sleeping, but when I lumber into the chair at the foot of her bed, she opens her eyes and welcomes me.

"Thanks for being here with me."

"It's the least I can do."

"Most people wouldn't be here with me out of fear. The world we live in is very secretive, and most people don't want to be seen outside of it. Sure, people see us on the streets, but that's where we live, and it's protected."

"Well, I'm new to this world, and I have nothing to hide. I couldn't just let you come alone."

"Are April and Ryle safe?"

"Bill is looking after them. They were hidden while the paramedics were there. We didn't want you getting into trouble or have them taken away from you."

"Oh, thank God." Marissa says with a deep sigh. "I was hoping someone would look out for us."

"Why wouldn't they?"

"I don't socialize with very many people in the group. They think I'm a snob, and that I don't care about the others. They think that I am using them by hiding in their world. I'm not hiding. I had nowhere else to go."

We chat for another half hour before she falls asleep again. I sit back in the chair, discovering it reclines, and fall asleep myself. As the morning light breaks the darkness in the room, I open my eyes. Marissa is still sleeping, and a nurse is taking her vitals. The nurse informs me that Marissa has pneumonia, and will have to stay at the hospital until she is better. There is no telling how long that will take.

After Marissa wakes up and has her breakfast, I leave the hospital and go to give our group an update. When I arrive at the stronghold under the freeway, Henry is the only one there. I don't know where the others collect their earnings. Using some paper and some burnt wood from the night's fire. I write a note to Elijah to let him know what is going on. I collect my belongings and head back to the hospital. I won't spend the night again, but I will stay with Marissa every day during her stay at the hospital. During our time together I learn a lot about her, and we become very good friends.

Marissa

Marissa was born on a farm on the border of Iowa and Illinois, literally, the border went straight down the middle of her family's farm. She was born three weeks early, and her mother didn't make it to the hospital in time. Marissa was born on the laundry room floor while her father worked in the field harvesting that season's corn. When her father came back to the house he was astonished and rushed Marissa and her mother to the hospital. During the birth Marissa's mother experienced severe hemorrhaging. She never left the hospital. Marissa's father was devastated at the loss of his wife. For months he mourned her, and his sister took care of Marissa. The years after that he was very distant from Marissa. He did all of the things' fathers are supposed to do, but in his care, he was devoid of emotion towards her. Marissa knew he loved her, but he didn't know how to express it. She was depressed through her teenage years, and had attempted suicide several times. She experimented with drugs and alcohol to try and feel alive. The only thing that did was make her forget for a while, but life and the past always seemed to find her again. She managed to graduate high school and got accepted to a local community college. She earned her associates degree with a certificate in medical billing and coding.

It wasn't easy finding a job in her town of 150 people, so she decided to pack up and head to Chicago. The little money she had was barely enough to pay her rent for a few months. She was able to find a job in her field, but rent was still expensive and difficult to pay on her own. She put up a note on the staff bulletin board letting people know that she was interested in getting a roommate. Several people were interested and came by to check out the apartment, but it was Marcus who would win her over. Although Marissa had no interest in a romantic relationship with Marcus, things between them developed. Everything was great for a while. They did everything together. Marcus was transferred to another branch of the company on the other side of the city, and Marissa was promoted to department head. This is when everything started to fall apart. Marcus became jealous and started to suspect Marissa of cheating on him. He checked the text messages on her cell phone. He read her emails and anything that was sent to her on social websites. She had no privacy. The more she denied cheating on him the more paranoid he became.

It was the day before Easter on their second year together. Marissa had just come home from work and Marcus was waiting for her in the living room. When she came in the door, she immediately noticed that he was intoxicated. Marcus was just standing there with his arms to his side looking at her. He didn't say anything to her, but he followed her every movement with his eyes. She tried talking to him and asked him questions. He never said a word to her. She finally got fed up and walked past him to go into the bedroom to change clothes. Marcus grabbed her. He forced her into the bedroom. He ripped off her clothes and raped her.

While Marcus was passed out Marissa went to the police. She told them her story. She went to the hospital to have a rape kit done, but because she and Marcus had been intimate for years it was hard to prove rape. Marcus was arrested, but the charges were dropped due to lack of evidence. An order of protection was placed against Marcus, but he continued to harass Marissa. She feared for her life. She moved to another apartment to try and get away, but he managed to find her again. She was walking to work on a day that she was supposed to have off, and Marcus surprised her just before she got to work. It was then that he noticed the size of her abdomen. She was pregnant with twins, and they were his. Marcus ran away crying.

It wasn't until a year after the twins were born that she saw Marcus again. He had cleaned up his act and had sought help for his alcohol and abuse problems. He apologized for what he had done. He knew he could not expect forgiveness from Marissa, but he had to tell her he was sorry. He managed to win his way back into her life over the next few months. He was a good father for about three years, but then he got fired from his job. April and Ryle were four years old by then, and Marcus stayed home to watch them while Marissa was at work. He had started drinking heavily and had discovered drugs. The last time Marissa and the twins saw him he was in the back seat of a police car being taken away for tying Marissa to the bed and continually beating and raping her for three days. Thankfully, Brianna, a friend from work noticed that Marissa had been gone without telling anybody or calling in. She came to Marissa's apartment and heard the twins crying. She heard Marissa cry out in pain as Marcus pounded his fist into her face.

Brianna called the police, and Marissa was saved. Marcus was only sentenced to eight months in jail. Due to overcrowding, he was released after serving only three months. It was then that Marissa took her children and disappeared into an invisible world. That was two years ago. She has been hiding ever sense.

A Special Birthday

After four days in the hospital Marissa is released to go home. I fill her prescriptions and walk her home. Everyone is glad to be reunited with her especially April and Ryle. I had kept everybody informed about what was going on with Marissa after my hospital visits. Although I visited her every day, I did have to earn a living. I usually went to the hospital around seven every morning and stayed until lunch. I then proceeded to my claim to earn my wage for the day. The twins were sent to school every day, and they were looked after every night by the group. Marissa is in tears after finding this out because she now knows that everybody cares.

I've been living on the streets for a week now, but with all that has happened this week it seems like it has been much longer. Not only do I feel welcomed by my "neighbors", but I also feel accepted into their family. Today is my birthday, and somehow Elijah found this bit of information out and decided to throw me a party. I'm surprised when I wake up to everybody singing *Happy Birthday* to me. Elijah is standing over me with a six-pack of cupcakes with a candle in each one. Bill is cooking omelets for everybody, and Harvey is cooking bacon. Eric and Victor are buttering and toasting bread. Everybody has managed to pitch in and get me a package of socks and a package of T-shirts as a gift. To the average person this might not seem like much, but the thought of people I have only known for a week spending all of their meager earnings and throwing me a birthday party is overwhelming. Not many people will ever know this, but in my 37 years on this earth, this is the first time I've ever had a birthday party. Rough childhood you would think, but it's more like my family didn't celebrate mundane things like birthdays.

After the delicious breakfast and celebration, we all go about our day. I head out to my sidewalk claim in front of Dylan's Candy Bar, but I'm quickly turned around when I see people who know me for who I really am. I'm not ready to explain myself, and they would never understand my explanation anyway. I decide to head further up Michigan Avenue and find a new claim. I walk by the huge statue of Marilyn Monroe and am amazed by how many people find this statue interesting. I cross the street to the Wrigley building and find a place to perch myself. As I get my sign and coffee cup out, I notice a little boy standing about ten feet away from me staring at me.

"Hello"

"Why're you sitting on the ground?"

"Sometimes the ground is the only place to sit."

"Why're your cloths so dirty?"

"I've been working really hard."

"What do you do?"

"That's kind of hard to explain."

"My Dad is a financial consultant in London. That is where we live, London. We came to Chicago for Holiday"

"London is a beautiful city. How do you like Chicago?"

"It's cold. Where we live it doesn't snow as much."

"That's one thing we get a lot of here, snow."

Before the young lad can say anything else his parents come to his side and ask what he is doing.

"I am talking to that nice man there," he says as he points to me.

"Well let's be going then. Good day to you sir." The father says as he puts a $20 bill in my cup."

The boy waves to me as he and his parents walk further along the avenue.

I'm not one to brag, but I think I have found the spot I'm going to claim as my own for the remainder of my excursion. I have collected over $500 today. For the past week I was fortunate enough to collect $80 to $100 each day. Elijah said I'd be lucky to collect $20. I have been living off of $40 each day and saving the rest. The money we make each day is never discussed amongst the group because, even though we are a family, money would get stolen. The longer walk to Millennium Park hurts more than usual. Being further away and walking longer makes the stiff joints and sore muscles I've acquired after sitting in one place for an entire day scream in rebellion. I head to the store as usual and get food. While at the store I decide to grab some muscle rub. I don't want to sound like I'm weak, but the pain I'm experiencing is no joke.

The evening is filled with fun and laughter. *Happy Birthday* is sung to me several more times throughout the night, and it seems to me that my special day has brought out a few extra bottles of whiskey. Thankfully I don't indulge in the alcohol because I have taken a few too many painkillers, and I think the mixture might kill me. As I wrap my thoughts around the day's happenings, I find myself drifting off into the world of slumber. Before I know it, the painkillers take over my body. I fall into a deep sleep

I'm jolted awake by someone kicking me in the side. Not hard enough to hurt me, but just enough to make me almost pee myself in fear of not knowing what is going on. I jump to my feet and run behind a support pillar to relieve my bladder. Nobody questions what I'm doing because urinating behind the pillars is not only frequently done by all, but it's an acceptable practice when so few bathrooms are accessible to people living in our situation. I walk back over to my bed area to find out what my sleep murderer wants. Eric is standing with his head down and is lightly kicking around a large piece of ice.

"Hey Eric. Sorry I had to run off like that. You scared the pee out of me, literally. What's up?"

"Well, nothing really…I kinda need someone to talk to before it's too late. I thought you might want to listen to what I gotta say."

"You want to tell me something? Why me? Before what is too late?"

"Hell, I don't know. You seem different than everybody else, and I thought you wouldn't mind if I got something off of my chest."

"I am all ears buddy. Do you want to sit or should we walk somewhere else?"

"I guess we should walk. I don't want the others to overhear us, and…I don't know…I guess I just want things to be private…you know…just in case."

"I think I understand. Let's walk."

Eric

Eric has been living on the streets for many years. He never dreamed he would end up where he is today. Eric holds an MBA, but he only got to use it for a few years before he ended up getting himself into a bit of trouble. Eric worked with a firm in Manhattan that managed accounts for foreign owned companies operating in the US. Living a life of luxury, Eric somehow found his way into the world of heroin and other drugs. He used frequently, and every dime he made went to funding his habit. The more he used, the more his finances suffered. He began syphoning money from the accounts he managed into his own privately owned account. It took two years for the company to notice, but by the time they did Eric had quit the company and walked away with all of the money. He was careful not to leave a paper trail implicating him. The company had no grounds to charge him with a crime, although, they knew Eric was the one who had embezzled the money. Yet his addiction soon overcame his judgement.

Feeding a habit, and using up all of his stolen money, Eric found himself breaking into houses and stealing whatever he could flip for quick cash. It didn't take long for him to become suspected by the police. Eric relocated to Illinois to avoid prosecution in New York. When he arrived in Chicago, he sold his car and the few belongings he had brought with him. With the little money he had he sought out someone to help fuel his habit. Being new to the area he had a hard time locating what he was looking for. Eric managed to get himself into rehab via state insurance, but it wasn't to get himself free of his addiction. Eric used his time in rehab to find the names and locations of drug dealers from other patients. After he got the information he needed, he checked out early and went under the radar.

It was a warm summer day when Eric was surprised by a homeowner as he was robbing a house. A woman walked in to find her house a mess from Eric searching for sellable items. He was in the hallway when she walked into the living room. He ducked into a bedroom and prayed she would walk outside to call the police, allowing him to escape through the bedroom window. The homeowner did just the opposite. She walked down the hall towards the bedroom Eric was hiding in. As she rounded the door to the room Eric was hiding in, he hit her in the head with a lamp, sending her flailing onto the floor. Eric took what he could and ran out the back door.

It was several days later when Eric saw a police sketch of himself on the news. He learned then that the woman he hit in the head was dead. Knowing there was no way out of being charged with murder; Eric decided to hide on the streets. He knew the police wouldn't look for him in the homeless huts under the freeway. At least he hoped they wouldn't.

A few days ago, Eric tells me, he spotted someone lurking around his collection post. The stranger stared at Eric and watched his every move. When Eric got up to leave for the day the stranger talked into his wrist detective style and followed him. Being an expert at losing people Eric managed to avoid and lose the stranger. He knew it wouldn't be long before he would be found. Eric decided to tell me his story. It wasn't because he wanted to be remembered. It wasn't because he was proud of what he'd done. He told me his story because he was ashamed. Killing the woman was not intentional, but he knew it was murder all the same. He couldn't live with the guilt anymore, and he needed to get things off his chest.

Deep Freeze

"Freeze! Get your hands where we can see them! I said FREEZE!"

Police are swarming our neighborhood. They stand with guns fixed on Eric. There are at least 30 police officers standing in the open and also behind squad cars. Eric takes off running. A few shots are fired in his direction, but they cease quickly because I'm in the line of fire. Several police officers slam me to the ground and put me in handcuffs. Not knowing what to do, I comply. I know they are not here for me and will let me go once they identify that I'm not a threat.

Several minutes pass, and the police are communicating through shoulder radios. Officers have spotted Eric and are on the chase. Eric has somehow managed to get up to the freeway and is running with traffic trying to avoid being caught. As he gets above us, he climbs the traffic barrier and looms on the edge. He appears to have a gun pointed to his head. Police officers have stopped traffic and are focused on Eric. They're yelling for him to step down. He holds the object to his head and yells back to them. I can't understand what he's saying, but I don't think he's surrendering.

I look down for a second so I can adjust my sitting position. Sitting on cold concrete in handcuffs is not comfortable. As I look up again, I see Eric. He is flying like an auk towards the ground in slow motion. It isn't long after his flight begins that a loud thud is heard as Eric's plummet suddenly comes to an end.

I'm taken to the local precinct for questioning. It takes longer to explain to the police my true identity and the reason behind my excursion than it does to convince them that I know nothing about Eric. I'm finally released after four hours of brutal questioning. I leave the precinct and walk back to my neighborhood. It's quiet. The police tape has been removed. The blood stains from Eric's demise have been covered by old blankets and cardboard. Nobody is around. When the police pay a visit, everybody seems to disappear. I don't know where everybody is sleeping, but only Elijah, Henry, and I remain in the neighborhood. Elijah keeps near Henry and does not say anything to me. I respect his need for silence and keep to myself.

The temperature drops well below freezing while I sleep. I'm woken up by the shivering of my body. Somehow my hat has managed to wiggle itself off of my head. I locate it near my pillow and put it back on. I pull the hoods of the several hoodies I am wearing up over and around my head. I pull the strings tight and tie them so they don't come loose. I can't seem to fall back to sleep. The cold air hurts the back of my throat and my lungs as I breathe it in. I look over to where Elijah and Henry are. They seem to be sleeping comfortably. I guess they have become immune to the weather after having had to live on the streets for so many years.

I decide to get up. It is around 2 o'clock in the morning. I know there is a convenience store open 24 hours, but it will be a long cold walk for me just to get a warm cup of coffee. The streets are dead. There isn't a single person or car out and about the streets of Chicago. I've never seen any city this quiet. It's an eerie sight. First Eric dies, and everyone in the neighborhood disappears. Then the cold chases everyone out of the city. An unsettling feeling comes over me. I don't know what it is, but I can't get my uneasiness to subside. I begin to walk faster. The night seems to confine me. I feel overwhelmed by the darkness. The cold is cutting through me. I'm trying to walk, but I can't seem to move. It feels like I'm tied up. I feel a wetness dripping down my skin under my clothes. Suddenly I feel someone grab me. Elijah is kneeling beside me as I realize I'm waking from a nightmare.

"You alright Craig? I heard you screaming in your sleep. I've been trying to wake you for about 10 minutes."

"Elijah? I thought I was awake already. You sure I was sleeping?"

"I have been here all night. Haven't been able to sleep because of the cold. Well, that and after what happened this afternoon. Scared the hell out of me."

"Could be why I had a nightmare. I was dreaming that I was walking around through the city and it was abandoned. Creepy feeling came over me. I...I can't explain it."

"Been there. I know the feeling well. Seems to happen to all of us at least once in our lives. Especially those of us living the way we do."

Elijah and I walk to the store to get some coffee since neither of us can get back to sleep. The streets are not deserted, but there are very few cars out. The coffee soothes our nerves and dispels the cold from our bones.

I find my place on the sidewalk to collect my offerings for the day. It's Monday, and despite the below zero temperatures there are quite a few people walking out and about. My coffee cup quickly gets full, and I have to empty it several times within the first half-hour. The day continues to prove profitable. I will tell you that, although, I have made a lot of money today, it will not be the highest profits I make in one day.

I head away from my spot as the sun starts to lower in the sky. I go buy myself coffee and food to share. I'm not sure how much food to buy since yesterday nobody was around. I realize that I haven't eaten in the past two days. Coffee doesn't count as food. I buy the usual grub and head to the meeting place our group gathers so we can travel home together. I'm stunned when I see that our group has grown rather large today. I wedge my way into the crowd unnoticed, and hide away amongst the other people. Elijah spots me and winks in my direction. He knows what I'm doing.

I discover the reason for our rather large gathering tonight. Several areas where the homeless live have been closed down by authorities due to severe weather. Many areas of the city where homeless are known to live are monitored by police and other authorities to prevent death amongst us. Authorities try and force us into staying in shelters. Too many people refuse to stay in shelters because they have secrets they choose not to share. At shelters people have to give their name and other information in order to receive assistance. I've avoided these shelters because I want to survive the true hardships of living homeless. If I die during my adventure, then so be it.

Fortunately, other neighborhoods share many of the same characteristics as ours, and there is enough food to share with everyone. It's good to have new stories to hear, and have new people to experience life with for the night. The pain of yesterday subsides, but a tinge of memory is felt as our guests discuss what they heard through the grapevine about the situation. When they realize the effect their discussion has on us, they quickly change the subject. A group of musicians helps forget the cold with good music, good food (well at least food), and to those who partake, good drink.

The next day goes by without incident. The weather takes an even colder turn, and many of our guests decide that the shelters are their best chance of survival. Marissa and the kids, along with Elijah, Henry, Bill, Harvey, Victor, and I take the challenge and remain exposed to the elements. Shelters ask many questions about who a person is and will sometimes turn to authoritative figures if they feel a person is in danger or putting someone else in danger. Because Marissa fears losing her children, she avoids shelters. Marissa, April, and Ryle set up camp next to me. After the ordeal Marissa went through with pneumonia, she feels safer moving closer to the rest of us. She chose to move next door to me because we connected when I stayed with her at the hospital. April and Ryle are happy because they think I saved their mom. I warned them that Bill, my other neighbor, snores really loudly. They say they don't mind because I'll take care of them.

Since Marissa, April, and Ryle have moved in next door to me we decide to build a house for them. We gather boxes and blankets of different sizes and attempt to construct a monumental three-bedroom mansion. Bill and a few others pitch in, and the only thing we accomplish is to get into an awesome pillow fight.

As the night settles in I sit back and admire the liveliness of everyone. It seems as though we are celebrating. There is no special occasion to celebrate, but we don't need one. We are glad to be alive. We are happy just to be able to survive in such harsh conditions. We are thankful for each other.

Living vs. Having

I'm only at the beginning of the second week of my adventure. I have witnessed death, been bitten by Mother Nature, and have had the pee scared out of me. Most people would have quit by now, but I will persevere. I feel closer to the people I have lived with for the past few weeks than I do to people I have known my entire life. Although I am surrounded by heavy drinkers and people on drugs; there is just something about living on the streets that changes the priorities of a person's life. I trust these people with my safety and my life. I know that, although, we haven't shared all aspects of our lives, the men, women, and children with whom I'm surrounded have become a sort of family to me. They will protect me unquestionably as I would do for them.

As the sun dissipates the night sky its rays reflect off of the snow and make the morning glow. I eat my breakfast with my friends and then walk the kids to school with Marissa. When we arrive at the school, I notice the look on the faces of the administrators. They know the situation in which we live, but they are too ashamed of us to do something about it. Thankfully April and Ryle are able to have an occasional sponge bath in a random restroom to keep them from smelling, but the cleanliness and state of their clothes allows the other children to make fun of them. I'm not sure what Marissa does to keep clean, but that isn't something that one talks about. "Where do you take a shower so you don't stink at work?" Not a conversation I really want to start. I'm glad that April and Ryle have the strength to ignore the taunting and bullying from the other children. When my month is over, I promise myself to help Marissa and the children every way that I can.

Marissa and I walk towards her job. Her coworkers don't know her situation because she keeps her personal life quiet at work, but her coworkers do know that she is hiding something. If they knew the magnitude of Marissa's secrets, they would probably shun her. I don't know what it is about society that they feel the need to think poorly of the poor. Just because a person does not have money doesn't mean they are subhuman. Unfortunately, not everyone understands this.

I settle into my collection post and notice all of the people walking around me. Although I have sat many days on the sidewalk surrounded by people, I have never noticed the people. Of course, I have seen them, but I haven't really paid attention to their activities. I'm amazed about how many people are clueless of each other. I'm not amazed that they are clueless concerning my presence. I know that the people walking past me see me, but they pretend I'm invisible. Even the people who toss a few coins or dollar bills into my cup seem blind towards me. They are consumed by talking on cell phones, making deadlines at work, and taking care of themselves and their families. The most important thing in their lives is having more and better things, consuming every object produced. They are consumed by the quest for consuming more. What they don't know is that there is more to life than that. They are oblivious to what life is about. Life is about living not having. Maybe I am generalizing about everybody in society, but in my real life, consumption is normal practice.

Living in my house surrounded by all of my materialistic possessions spoiled me. Sitting here on the streets cold, hungry, and unbathed makes me realize that I took my life for granted. There is enough wealth around that nobody should ever have to live on the streets. Granted, there are those who choose to live in this fashion. The world will never be rid of poverty, but if more people would live a simpler life and help those in need there would be much less suffering. I know that when I go back to my materialistic possessions, I will keep what I have. I have learned to live without in two short weeks, and I will continue to follow through with simple living. Not to the extreme of simplicity that I am living now, but I won't be going out and buying every new gizmo and gadget that comes up for sale.

Harvey

I get up after a long day of sitting and collecting money. I spot Harvey walking towards

me. He is smiling from ear-to-ear.

"Hey Craig! What's up?"

"Just another day at the grinding stone. You?"

"Well, I'm excited. Wanna know why? Do ya, do ya? Come on ask me why I'm excited."

"Why are you excited, Harvey?"

"I got a job. I've been in and out of job interviews for over a year now. Most places turn

me down because I'm not dressed properly. Well today that changed. I was up on the 45th floor

of this building and waiting my turn. The secretary was looking at me and she kept spraying air

freshener in my direction. She didn't think I noticed, but I did. The boss man came out of his

office and looked me over. He said, 'Why are you dressed like a bum?' I told him, 'Because I've

been living on the streets for over a year. I haven't been able to find a job, and I lost everything

when I got laid off and my unemployment ran out.' He said, 'I think I need to interview you

then.' I was shocked that he still wanted to interview me. He said, 'There's no way in hell I

would every look at someone who looks like you and think you have what it takes to work here,

but I'm willing to give you a chance.' The interview was amazing. I gave him all of my

qualifications and my resume. He didn't want references because he was going with his gut on

this one. I impressed him, and I got the job. I start next week. He even took me shopping and bought me some clothing appropriate for work. I will have to pay him back out of my paychecks, but I'll be making enough it won't make a difference. You are now looking at the new 'Director of Human Resources.' What do you think of that?"

"Harvey! That's amazing! Congratulations!"

"I knew you would be proud. I'm not going to tell anybody else, but I had to tell someone. You seemed like the kind of guy who I could tell that to."

"Why don't you want anybody else to know?"

"Some of these guys will think I'm turning my nose up to them. They will start treating me like I'm a snob. Besides that, I will still have to live on the streets until I can get an apartment. I don't want them hating me because I have a job. You won't tell them, will you?"

"Harvey, I would never break your trust like that. I am really happy for you."

"Cool. Let's go get a bite to eat. Not at the store though. I want to go to a real restaurant. My treat."

"Well that sounds like a real treat, but it will be my treat. This is a celebration, and you never pay for your own party."

"Craig you are the greatest. Man, I feel great."

Harvey and I walk around the loop looking for a good place to eat. After eating spam, bread, and sardines since I've been on the streets, the menus are overwhelming. We finally decide on a simple diner style establishment, and we both order bacon cheeseburgers with fries and an iced tea.

Harvey lost his job as a production supervisor at a very prestigious manufacturing firm. He was successful, powerful, and wealthy. When the economy took a nosedive and corporate bureaucracy replaced common sense, Harvey lost everything he had worked for. He was able to get unemployment for a while, but it was nowhere near what he was making from his job. He searched for job after job, but was unsuccessful in finding anything. He applied at fast food restaurants, retail stores, and construction firms. He was turned away from all of them because he was overqualified. Holding a degree in business management, and having 22 years' experience as a corporate executive made potential bosses fear Harvey was only trying to take their job or would leave as soon as he found something better. This made it difficult for him to obtain anything. After struggling for a year or so Harvey finally sold his last possession, his home. He had sold off all of his other possessions little by little in order to survive, but being unable to find a job finally broke him. Because Harvey was not married and had no children, he made the ultimate sacrifice and became homeless.

Harvey's immediate family treated him as a failure after he lost his job. They refused to lend him any kind of support. Harvey is a very proud individual. He was taught by his family that he has to earn what is rightfully his. Some who have come from extreme wealth and then losing everything have a very humbling experience. Many who have come from extreme wealth and then lose it commit suicide. There were a few moments where he almost succumbed to this temptation, but he was strong enough to survive. His belief is, "He did it on his own once, and he can do it again."

Due to the rejection by his family, Harvey has decided not to have any contact with them again. Even after he gets back on his feet, he feels that his family isn't worth his time or effort. No matter how down a member of a family gets, it's the responsibility of the rest of a family to help take care of that person. That is what Harvey believes.

Harvey had never found that special someone. He tried to have a few relationships over the years, but for some reason they never seemed to work out. It wasn't because Harvey didn't try, but something just wasn't right with the women he dated. He didn't feel any real commitment or attraction to any of them. There were feelings for them, but he didn't love any of them. Something else filled his heart, but he could never put a name to it. He wasn't able to explore any of his true emotions or who he really was until he lost everything. With nothing to distract him he was able to search and understand his inner feelings. It was only after months of being alone with his thoughts and feelings that Harvey discovered why all of his relationships with women failed. He realized he was attracted to men. He has never acted upon his feelings, and he has never told anyone, other than me, his true feelings. Harvey hopes to one day find someone to love and start a family with. He understands that being in his late forties it is difficult to start a family, but now that Harvey has discovered who he really is, he realizes this is what he really wants. A family.

April

Sipping coffee and eating a piece of apple pie served with ice cream, Harvey and I are

utterly satiated. Full from our meal, we each take a box of leftovers – more than enough for

tomorrow. Living on the street and eating very little food has taken its toll on our bodies. Our

stomachs are not as big as they used to be. I hadn't noticed until now that I have lost quite a bit

of weight. I never thought I could lose weight this fast. The lack of food and shivering cold has

burned the fat off of my body. I will need to make sure I don't lose too much weight. In order to

survive this, I must keep my health.

Harvey and I head back to our area under the freeway. The others have already arrived.

We stopped to buy some food to share with everyone, but we have hidden our leftovers from

them. We are not ashamed that we have eaten out, but we don't want anybody giving us trouble

thinking we have money to spare. We may look out for each other's safety, but that doesn't mean

there aren't those among us who will rob us blind. They might even kill to get what they want. It

is a bit of a conundrum to feel safe amongst those who are willing to kill.

As the others eat their dinner Harvey and I snack a bit, but we sneak away and share our

leftovers with April and Ryle. They are very excited to eat even the remains of bacon

cheeseburgers and fries. It has been quite a while since they have eaten something other than

school food and the daily passing of beans and mystery meat. Marissa just sits back and smiles at

the kindness we have brought to her children. The children finish their food and are keeping themselves busy with homework. Marissa asks me if I want to go for a walk with her. Harvey and Bill agree to watch April and Ryle. We sneak away unnoticed by the rest of the group.

As we walk down the street Marissa begins to cry.

"Why are you so kind to me and the kids? You don't need to be. Nobody asked you to help us. So, tell me why you are doing it. What do you want?"

"Marissa, I don't want anything. I can't honestly tell you why I am helping you. I guess when you got sick, I saw your vulnerability, and I learned your story. There's a part of my heart that's too soft. I have an unexplainable desire to keep you and the kids safe."

"Well, I can't say it isn't appreciated." Marissa says with almost uncontrollable tears as she falls into my arms hugging me. "I don't know what it is about you, but I trust you. I've never trusted anyone since Marcus, and you know how that worked out for me. I'm scared Craig. Some part of me cares about you, and I don't want to be hurt by you. I don't think you could do something like that to me, but after my experiences you can understand my doubts. You aren't like anybody else here. You don't have a hardened heart. You never ask for anything after helping anybody. Everybody else here, with the exception of Elijah, wants something in return for helping someone out. I keep my distance because other groups I have tried to live with thought I was a sex toy. When I refused them, I got hit. Here nobody messes with me because they know Elijah will protect me. Elijah never helps anybody but Henry, but he won't let anybody get hurt here either. If you do something wrong, he will make you leave. Do you understand what I'm trying to say?"

"I don't know. I have an idea, but I don't want to say it and be wrong. If I am wrong what, I have to say might hurt you. If I am right, it will be the first time in my life this has happened to me."

"I can't say it. I refuse to until I know for sure. I don't want to make another mistake, and I refuse to put my kids through that again. I hope you can understand, and I hope you know what I am saying."

"I understand. I respect your decision."

"Thank you for caring, and thanks for everything."

Marissa gives me a kiss on the lips, but not an intensely passionate one. It's very reserved, but I understand the meaning behind it. She stops hugging me, and looks me deep in the eyes. I smile at her and wink. We both start walking back to our home. She takes my hand in hers, and we walk back in silence. As we approach what I've come to call "the neighborhood" she releases my hand after a light squeeze. Ryle needs my help with his spelling test, and April is reading. Bill and Harvey quietly walk to their houses. I end up falling asleep with Ryle in my arms and April leaning on my shoulder.

The morning air is frigid. A light dry snow fell during the night. Ryle is still in my arms when I awaken, and April has moved over with her mother. I quietly lay Ryle down as I try and get up. I cover him up with more blankets and make sure his head is covered. It's Saturday. The hustle and bustle of the city will begin in a few hours. I think I am going to do something special with Marissa and the kids today. I go to the store down the road and buy bacon, eggs, and English muffins. I find a cheap frying pan also. I pay for my items and head back to the neighborhood. When I arrive, I find everyone getting up for the day. I start to cook the food I bought, and the smell of the bacon has aroused those who have not yet gotten up. Everybody loves the smell of bacon.

"So, I'm thinking about doing something out of the ordinary today with you and the kids. You up for it?"

"What is it? Is that why you cooked such an awesome breakfast?"

"You see right through me don't you. I was thinking we could go to the Lincoln Park Zoo. I think the kids would get a kick out of that."

"Don't you need to earn some money today? You bought restaurant food yesterday, and after today's breakfast you must have spent a fortune."

"The zoo is free, and I'll be ok. I didn't spend that much. Besides, I did well the other day." (I can't even tell Marissa about the $500 I made the other day.)

"Alright. If you're sure. I think the kids will love it. I have avoided taking them places because I am scared Marcus will show up somehow."

"I don't think Marcus is the kind of man who goes to the zoo. Well, not after what you told me about him anyway. Especially in the middle of January."

"I know, but I still don't trust it. I'm willing to go though."

We get the kids bundled up in their winter gear, more than what they are already wearing, and head out. After walking for a while and idle chit-chat we find ourselves in front of the Art Institute. Both April and Ryle are fascinated by the giant lions guarding the entrance.

"Wow! That lion looks scary. Why is he there?"

"He is guarding the entrance to the art museum, Ryle. He is supposed to scare off art thieves."

"Craig, you're so weird. Can we go inside?"

"Well, we can at least go in and warm up."

April looks as excited as Ryle about going inside, so we decide to head in. The warm air is comforting as we walk past the grand doors into the awaiting lobby. We head in sheading a few hundred layers of clothing each. We're thrilled to find it's a free day. We can actually see the art.

We walk around the museum and look at all of the different exhibits. Marissa and the kids are in awe. I will admit that I'm impressed as well. We discuss quite a few of the pieces. April lingers longer than anyone looking at each piece. She concentrates. The magic in her eyes flow with every brush stroke. She devours every bit of knowledge she learns from the caption for each painting. Now Van Gogh's *Sunflowers*. Now Monet's *Cathedral*. Now Seurat's *Sunday in the Park*. She listens intently as I tell her about the way oils, acrylics, and watercolors come to life in the imagination of the artist. Her fascination grows when she learns the value of each piece. The museum proves to be a bigger hit than I could have ever imagined.

As we come out of the Art Institute, we walk across the street to a coffee shop. The kids get hot cocoa, and Marissa and I get some fancy coffee that costs more than an entire can that will make 90 cups. Oh well, it is a special occasion. We walk down the block and April spots The School of The Art Institute of Chicago. She stops in front of it and stares into the glass.

"How does someone go here?"

"You have to be accepted. Once you finish high school you apply. If they accept you, you can study here and earn your degree."

"But, what do you have to do?"

"You have to have the desire to go. If you have the desire, you will do it. It takes self-motivation and hard work. With those two things you can do anything you want, April."

"Cool."

We walk around Chicago for a few hours before we settle on a place for lunch. Thankfully we aren't turned away at the door for our unsightly appearance. Marissa is worried about being out in public with her children, always concerned Marcus might spot them. We eat quickly and head out again. The day has gone by quickly, and the early sunset is approaching. It has gotten substantially colder than it was when we left out this morning. The wind has picked up and the night is steadily becoming miserable. The thrill of being out and about on the weekend has worn off. The kids are starting to get cranky.

We gather by the fire with everybody else. The wind is blowing so hard the heat from the fire doesn't seem to reach us. We give up after a few minutes. The children gather up all of their blankets and curl up underneath them. I curl up in my sleeping bag and turn so I can see the kids. Marissa grabs her blankets and a sleeping bag and curls up behind the kids. A van pulls up on the outskirts of our neighborhood and a few people climb out. They start handing blankets to everybody. Marissa, Bill, Harvey, and I hide the children. They approach us and give us a few blankets each, a large coffee, and a cup of soup. We are offered shelter at one of the local homeless shelters, but we thank them and politely refuse.

Once the charity groups leave, April emerges from her blanket bungalow. Ryle has fallen asleep. April has a notebook in her hand and she nudges it towards me. I take it from her and she burrows back into her blankets. I spend the rest of the night sleepless. What she has handed me is a book of drawings. Not just any drawings. Her drawings. There are immaculate pictures of every person in our group. There are portraits of her teacher at school. Several drawings of each person. All of them at different times, and all of them drawn without the subject's knowledge. I look at each drawing intently over and over again. Just to think, these drawings are from a six-year-old. I haven't noticed the tears frozen to my cheeks. I'm startled as April lays her head on my shoulder.

"What do you think? Ya think it is good enough to get in the school?"

"April. These are amazing. These are more than enough to get you into the school. Have you shown them to anybody else? Your mother?"

"No. I don't want anybody to know. I want it to be our secret. You promise?"

"I promise I won't tell anyone."

The biting wind has subsided, and the air has warmed from yesterday. The sun is hidden behind clouds that look like they are going to start sifting snow on us any minute. I tuck April back into bed. I skip breakfast and head out for the day. I'm not one to turn to religion, but I stop at a church and go inside. Votive candles are lit everywhere, and there are a few people kneeling in the pews. I walk to the front of the church and look up at the enormous crucifix hanging on the back wall behind the pulpit. Tears fill my eyes as I think about Marissa and the kids. I make a promise to God to always take care of them no matter what. I'm not sure how I'm going to do this, but I will make it happen.

Knocked Conscious

I walk to my claim not really interested in doing anything productive today. As I approach the bridge on Michigan Ave crossing over the Chicago River, I am stopped by police officers. They are not here to harass me, but keep me back from the commotion on the bridge. I see emergency crews and police officers on the bridge and along the river walk under the bridge. There are boats in the water, and a few divers are suiting up to search the river. Apparently, a young mother decided that it would be better if she were no longer around. This makes me think more about Marissa. She'll do anything for April and Ryle. I know she would die for them if it meant their survival, but I know that she would never kill herself.

What could drive a mother to end her life? Why would any mother not want to be there for her child? I'm not a mother, or even a woman for that matter, but if I were a father I would always want to be there for my children. I'm already dedicated to April and Ryle, and I've only known them for two short weeks.

I walk down the street to another bridge in order to cross the river. I don't want to be a spectator to the events that have unfolded, and I don't want to be noticed either. It's bitter cold out, but my brisk walk has caused me to sweat under my layers of clothing. I'm hoping I don't get sick.

The rest of the day is numb to me. I remember getting to my spot on the cold sidewalk, and now it's dark. Somehow, I absent mindedly let the day pass me by. My thoughts dwell on my life thus far and what has led me to be where I am now. I know I'm here to gain an insight on the life of the homeless so I can tell their stories, but I don't know what has happened to make me feel unfulfilled. I live to write, and I yearn to express myself through the written word. I have been very successful with my writing, and I've made a respectable living. Yet it's not enough. Marissa doesn't know who I am, and I hate lying to her. But I don't even know who I am anymore. I'm a pariah of my own making.

Bill is standing at his sleeping area when I arrive back to the neighborhood. Only a few people have gone out today because of the bitter cold. Nobody met me at the park as we usually do. I'm not sure why until I walk over to Bill.

"You might want to stand back. Henry's having one of his days. He's been trying to fight everybody he sees. Elijah has managed to keep him calm for a while now, but there's no telling when he may go nuts again."

"Is that why nobody went out today? Were they all here trying to help?"

"I guess that's what it was. I didn't go because it's too cold for me today. My old bones can't handle this weather."

"You didn't miss anything out there. Slow day. Well, some lady jumped into the river, but other than that nothing happened."

"Why is it people choose not to live. Hell, I prefer this life over not living. It's a sad world we live in."

"And it gets worse every day. Where are Marissa and the kids?" I say as I notice they aren't around.

"Marissa doesn't like the kids to see Henry in one of his fits. She says it's bad for their psyche. Whatever that means. I think she took them to the store. They should be back soon."

I settle myself in for the night, and begin to prep the food I bought to share. Tonight, is a hotdog with chili night. I figure since it is cold, we need something that is going to be with us for a while. I get my little sauce pan out to start heating the chili. I'm suddenly hit in the head with a large piece of ice. Henry is going at it again. He is yelling incoherently and throwing anything he can get his hands on. My vision is starting to get blurry. I can feel a warm oozing coming from the top of my head and flowing down the side of my head. My knit cap is soaked with blood, no longer able to hold back the river flowing from the large gash in my head.

I'm dizzy. My vision keeps going in and out. I hear Bill saying something, but I'm no longer able to understand anything he is saying. Silence and darkness overtake me.

I wake briefly in the back of an ambulance.

The sight of a bright light floods my eyes as I come to again. A mask-covered-face hovering over me greets me.

"Ah, you're awake. You took quite a blow to the head, Mr. Mueller. But, you're in the emergency room now. I have to staple the wound shut, but you will recover quite easily."

"I don't care about how fast I heal doctor. I just want to know how long it will take for the headache to go away." I manage to mumble semi-coherently.

"That all depends on you. If you get plenty of rest and keep warm for the next few days it should go away in the next day or so. I'll give you some really good pain killers too."

"Keep them. I don't take pain medication. Can't. Pushing fluids. That helps with headaches."

"Just to let you know we did an x-ray, and there are no fractures. There doesn't seem to be any cranial pressure either. Just a good knock on the head, and it caused your body to react by passing out. I do have one question for you though. Has your head always been shaped like an egg?"

"No, but it just likes to crack like one. I do have something I need to tell you when you are finished shaving and stapling my noggin. If it could be private that would be better."

"We can meet in my office once the nurse finishes your paperwork."

"Needs to be before that actually."

"Brianna, could you please excuse us for a second."

"Not a problem doctor."

"What is so important Mr. Mueller?"

"My name is not Craig Mueller."

I explain my situation and my true identity.

"That is one heck of a predicament to be in. Can you autograph one of your books for my wife?"

"Sure, as soon as I get back home."

I stop by the store to get my antibiotic prescription filled before I head back to the neighborhood. I also grab a new knit cap and a gallon of orange juice, but I realize I only have enough money for one of those. I have reached my $40 limit for the day. I go with the hat. As I leave the store, I take a pill. I also pull the label off of the bottle so nobody knows my real name. The walk back to the neighborhood is interrupted by Bill.

"Hey Craig, I was just headed to the hospital to see how you're doing."

"I was released about a half hour ago. I was just heading back home."

"So, what's the diagnosis? Did Henry's ice break your psyche?"

"Too funny. Nope. Just seven staples in my head."

"Ouch. That sucks."

"The freight train doing high-speed loops in my head hurts worse."

"Lean on me if you need to. We have a long walk back."

Bill

Bill was born and raised in a small town in western England. He was close to his parents and siblings. He worked as a shop keeper at his father's store until he moved away to go to college. Bill decided to marry a woman he met in college during his senior year. His family loved her, his friends loved her, and Bill loved her. They shared their lives with each other. Bill found a job working as an executive for a department store. Jackie, Bill's wife, worked as an elementary school teacher. They wanted to raise a family of their own, but Jackie was unable to bear children of her own. Jackie decided that she didn't want to adopt because if she could not have children of her own it wasn't meant to be. Bill felt it best not to push the issue, and he forgot about having a family. This decision seemed to put Bill and Jackie's marriage into slow motion. Daily life fell into a routine that was rarely broken. Somehow Jackie and Bill ended up sleeping in separate bedrooms. Jackie blamed Bill's robust snoring. Both knew that there was no passion in their marriage, but neither wanted to admit it. Bill had never really felt comfortable with Jackie. He loved her, but he never fell in love with her. He married out of what he felt was duty, and provided for her like he was taught.

It was an early spring morning when Bill found his passion. He was driving to work and saw a few prostitutes walking along the sidewalk. One particular prostitute stood out to Bill. He was a young man in his early 20's. Bill was shocked that he could not suppress his feelings for this young man. Bill thought he was very handsome, and he wanted to stop and talk to the young man. He resisted his urges and continued on to work. Later that evening, when on the way home, Bill saw the young man again. He admired him as he passed by. This went on for several weeks. Bill finally stopped one evening and asked the young man to get in his car. The young man introduced himself as Rico. Bill asked what his fee was, and Rico told him a variation of services and prices. They drove to a local hotel, and Bill paid Rico. Bill only wanted to talk to Rico. No services were provided other than conversation. Every few days Bill picked up Rico, and the same process took place. After a month Rico asked why they never did anything sexual. Bill said that he just wanted to talk. Rico took off his clothes and tried to seduce Bill. Bill backed himself to a wall and just stood looking at Rico. Rico asked if Bill wanted to do anything, and bill said he just wanted to look.

Jackie started to wonder what was going on with Bill. A person could set a clock on Bill's routine. He was home by five-thirty. He and Jackie ate dinner. They watched the news together. They went to their bedrooms to read. They went to sleep.

Bill wasn't coming home until late in the evening. He would call and say he was working late and would miss dinner. As these behaviors continued Jackie became suspicious. She knew that there was something going on with Bill long before he ever started coming home late. She knew there was something "off" with him. She couldn't quite put a finger on it though.

It was late one night, and Bill hadn't arrived home yet. Jackie took her car and went looking for him. She saw his car at the hotel, and she stopped down the street to observe. When Bill came out of the room with Rico, she knew what it was that had been bugging her all of these years about Bill. She discovered that he was gay. When Bill came home that night Jackie confronted him.

After Jackie confronted Bill, he decided to divorce her and live the way he wanted. He divided up their assets and decided to move to Chicago. Although Bill and Rico had never been passionate, they made a connection. Bill asked Rico if he would like to join him. Rico jumped at the opportunity. When they arrived in the Windy City, they were astounded by everything. Americans were nothing like they expected. People were more open about sexuality. They had facial piercings and tattoos. Their hair was every shade possible, and in many different styles. In England people looked the same, but something about starting over new in Chicago made things seem that much different.

Two months into their new lives, Bill and Rico were living together in a small apartment overlooking Lake Michigan. Rico was working as a waiter at a restaurant, and Bill was managing a retail clothing store. Bill thought everything was perfect. It wasn't until he discovered multiple unexplained charges on his credit cards that Bill woke up. He called Rico to ask if he knew what the charges were. Rico denied knowing anything.

Bill came home after work and discovered that Rico had moved out. After Bill called, Rico knew that his scam would be discovered. Rico had been stealing money from Bill since they arrived in Chicago. Bill's checking and saving accounts were depleted. He had no money. He had his job though, and he could make it living in Chicago on his own. What Bill didn't know was that Rico had syphoned money from the store Bill was managing. When Bill came in to work the next day he was brought into the office and fired. No charges were filed because they did not have definitive proof that he was the one who took the money, but because he was responsible for the store, he was responsible for the loss.

Bill tried to find another job, but nobody wanted to hire him due to the circumstances of being fired from his last job. It didn't take long for Bill to lose his apartment. He ended up on the streets, and he has been here for about a year. He is trying to save up enough money to buy a plane ticket and go back to England, but he is too ashamed to face his family.

Ryle

We get back home and Bill helps me into my sleeping quarters. My head is pounding, and I can hardly concentrate on anything other than going to sleep. I'm tormented by nightmares all night. I feel pressure and tightness on my chest as I wake up. I think that I am tangled in my clothing or sleeping bag. As I open my eyes and clear them from sleep, I find the reason for the pressure and tightness on my chest. While I was sleeping a rather large, fluffy, long-haired cat found shelter within my sleeping bag. I hear the twins giggling as I make my discovery.

"Good morning kitty cat. Do you mind moving so I can get out of my sleeping bag and start my day?"

The cat stretches and yawns. She then makes her way to the twins for some petting. I climb out of my makeshift house and get ready for the day. The twins play with the cat and Marissa shakes her head.

"Don't get too attached to that cat. You aren't keeping it, and more than likely it won't be here when I get off of work."

The twins laugh as the cat rolls over wanting a belly rub. I'm ready to start my day, but I have to quickly sit down. My head begins to spin. I feel like I'm going to throw up. I can't get my bearings. I decide to lie down on top of my blankets and sleeping bag to until the spinning subsides.

"Craig, are you alright? Your face just got really white and your eyes rolled up. It was like you was a Zombie or something."

"I'm OK, Ryle. I just need to lie down for a minute. When Henry hit me with that ice, I had no idea my head would be spinning for days afterward."

"We don't have school today cause of the cold. Me and April can take care of you all day if you ain't feeling good. Ain't that right April?"

"We can do that, and you can take care of our new cat. I named her Harriet. Mom says we can't keep her so we are giving her to you so you can take care of her for us. Isn't that nice of us?"

"Aren't you two sweet. Give me a few minutes, and I'll be right with you."

A few minutes pass as I lie on my bed. My head continues to spin. I feel like I am going to fall through the concrete. The doctor didn't think I had a concussion, but he said the swelling from the cut would cause pressure on my brain. I believe this to be the cause of the dizziness. Marissa brings a cup of coffee over to me.

"Lift your head up a bit and drink this. It isn't too warm. You need fluids. Might help the spinning to go away."

I sit up slowly and gently sip the coffee as Marissa holds the cup for me.

"I hear the kids don't have school today because of the cold. I can keep an eye on them if you want. I don't think I'm going to go out today."

"I was going to take the day off."

"Don't do that. You need to work. The kids volunteered to keep an eye on me today. I think I can handle them easily enough. I won't have to move much, and I know they have plenty of activities to keep themselves busy. We also have lots of blankets to keep us warm. Oh, and there's Harriet to keep them company."

"They aren't keeping that cat."

"But April says they're giving her to me so I can take care of her for them."

"You can watch the kids if you want. I won't argue with you. The cat is your choice."

"All will be well. Have a good day at work. Thanks for the coffee."

"You're welcome. Alright kids give me a hug and kiss goodbye. Be good for Craig. Don't you dare pester him too much. Make sure your homework is done, and do some reading or something. I will see you when I get back. Love you."

"Bye."

"Love you too mommy."

With that Marissa leaves for work and the twins come over to me. Ryle has a book, and April has her sketch pad. They sit on either side of me and look at me while I adjust myself to sit up. My head isn't spinning as bad as it was, and I know it will feel better once I get something to eat. I get some bread out of my stash and chew it slowly. Nothing like partially frozen bread for breakfast.

April is working on a drawing quietly. She hides it from me whenever I try to lean in and get a peek. Ryle is engrossed in his book, *James and the Giant Peach*, One of my favorite books as a child.

"What's going on in your book Ryle?"

"The peach just crossed the ocean?"

"That is one of the best parts. It gets exciting from there."

I'm amazed that a six-year-old is able to read and comprehend such an advanced book. When I was six, I could barely color between the lines let alone read a book like *James and the Giant Peach*.

The day gets colder as noon approaches. The twins and I are wrapped up in every blanket of theirs and mine. April is still drawing and Ryle is taking a nap. I have been James and his adventure with the peach since Ryle fell asleep. I set the book aside and wake up Ryle. It is time for lunch, and I get out some hot dogs and a can of baked beans. I put some paper and wood on the fire in the old oil drum and cook lunch. April eats slowly as she ponders her drawing, and Ryle devours his food as though he hasn't eaten in weeks. I barely nibble my food. My stomach churns as my dizziness returns. It isn't an overwhelming spin like it was this morning, but it's enough of an annoyance that I have to sit down again.

After lunch Ryle works on some homework. April always finishes her homework early so she doesn't have to worry about it. It isn't like they have much homework anyway. They are only in the first grade. April continues working on her drawing. Harriet is curled up in April's lap under the blankets. I have never seen such a young child stay on task for such a long time. Most children have very short attention spans. Everything is quiet until I hear a loud fart coming from my left.

"Ewwwww, Ryle that is so gross. You know you aren't supposed to fart in front of a lady."

"Ha ha ha. You ain't no lady, and real men fart when they want to. Ain't that right Craig?"

"Don't bring me into this. I am just trying to breath after smelling what just came out of your butt. Oh no, I think I am going to…to…die."

I fall over on my side and the twins laugh as they climb on top of me and chant in unison.

"He's dead. He's dead. We're free. We can run away now and take Harriet with us."

"Wait a minute. I think I'm alive."

I sit up and both April and Ryle run around screaming and laughing. I laugh to myself as I watch them play.

We decide to go for a short walk. The day has gotten colder, and it's supposed to get even colder as the night sets in. Hot cocoa and coffee inside of a warm coffee shop is much better than sitting on a pile of blankets in the cold, on cold concrete. April bundles Harriet up in my blankets and promises her that we will be back. Harriet just closes her eyes and goes to sleep. I wish I could sleep all day like a cat.

Our walk isn't long, and our visit to the coffee shop doesn't last long. After we get our drinks, we can't find a place to sit because it seems everybody in Chicago decided to visit the same coffee shop at the same time. We decide to drink them as we walk back to our houses. By the time we get back Ryle has finished his hot cocoa. April wants to finish hers while she reads a book. She thinks it will help keep her warm. My coffee got cold almost immediately after leaving the coffee shop. I chug the cold coffee and the three of us stand by the fire.

Once we have warmed ourselves enough to use the blankets again, we get out of the cold and bundle up. April gets a book and starts reading. Ryle curls up next to me and lays his head on my arm.

"Craig."

"Yes."

"Why aren't we like normal kids that live in houses?"

"Well, Ryle, that is a very tough question to answer."

"Mom says it's because bad people might find us and take me and April away from her."

"I think that your mother knows best. When she feels like you are not in danger anymore, she will find a place and you can live in a house like everybody else. How does that sound."

"I kinda like not being like everybody else, but not being cold and having a soft bed would be nice. I don't wanna watch TV or nothing like that. TV makes people dumb. You know that, right? I don't want to be dumb. I am smarter than other kids. Did you know that? My teacher says I read at a 4th grade level, but I have to work on my math. I don't even know what math is, but I am still smarter than other kids. April too. She is really smart even though she pretends not to be."

"I know that both of you are really smart. I'm glad that you know this. You know what's funny? I don't know what math is either."

We both laugh and then are quiet for a while. I listen to the few cars that pass overhead and watch Henry as he quietly mutters to himself.

"Do you think my daddy is going to find us and kill us?"

"What! Why do you think he would do that?"

"I read my mom's dairy. She writes in it all the time. She is scared that dad will find us and kill us. He might just kill her and take us away."

"Three things, Ryle. First, dairy is something that comes from cows, like milk. I think you mean diary. Second, I know that your mom will never let anything bad happen to you and your sister. Third, you shouldn't read someone's diary."

"I hope we don't get killed or taken away. I hear her cry at night when she thinks I'm asleep. I worry that she'll never be happy again. She's happy when she is around you."

"Being around all three of you makes me happy. You don't need to worry. Things are going to get better for all of you really soon."

"I hope so cause I hate being cold. How long have you been living in a box like us? We've been doing this since we were little. Before we started school. Mom used to sit by the train station with me and April, and people would put money in a cup for us. I see lots of people doing that. Mom doesn't do that anymore. She goes to work. She says she couldn't work before we was in school because she had to take care of us. One time April got real sick. She was hot and kept barfing all over the place. Mom cried for two whole days. I could hear her saying that she didn't want her baby to die. She loves us you know."

"I know that she loves both of you very much."

"Watch out! I gotta fart again."

We both get a good laugh from Ryle's fart, and April crinkles up her nose at us. Ryle goes to his construct of boxes and gets his book. He also grabs another book and hands it to me, *How to Make Choices You Won't Regret*. We sit back and read. I doze off.

"Mom! Ryle farted twice, and Craig encouraged him."

Marissa walks up to us and hugs both kids.

"It is nice to hear that he was so well behaved. Thank you, Craig, for watching them. I hope they weren't a burden. And I hope the smell wasn't too unbearable."

"All is well. They kept busy all day, and we went for hot cocoa and coffee. We ended up back here shortly because the place was packed. I hope you don't mind, but Ryle loaned me one of your books."

"It's the least I could do."

Marissa prepares dinner for me and the twins. This is the first time she has offered me something to eat since I have been here. I know that it's her way of paying me back for watching the kids. After we eat the kids curl into their beds and Marissa helps me change the bandage on my cut. I haven't noticed that the bandage is filled with dried blood. She finishes with the bandage and we each sit in the little areas we call home. We don't say anything to each other for the rest of the night. It's understood nothing needs to be said. I doze off to sleep without realizing that I have.

Victor

I wake up again with my head spinning, but not to the extent that it was yesterday. Harriet is curled up between my legs inside of my sleeping bag. How she managed to get that far into my bag baffles me. I'm just glad that I'm able to get out of my bed easily. The bitter winter air burns my throat as I take it into my lungs. I have never felt cold like this. Every muscle, joint, and bone in my body aches. My head throbs. The cold bores through me with its icy fingers.

I head to my collection spot. I notice that Victor has taken up a spot near me. Victor doesn't usually spend any time collecting money. He earns his money as a gay prostitute. I have talked to Victor on a few occasions while warming myself at the fire drums. Although we haven't spoken at length, Victor has been rather chatty with me recently.

I clear the snow and ice off the sidewalk, and sit on the cold concrete. Victor scoots himself closer to me. He offers me a milk crate to sit on. Why didn't I think of this before? No more numb butt.

"How's it going Craig?"

"Just another day in paradise."

"Understood. How's your head? Henry hit you pretty good the other day with that ice."

"My head is thicker than I thought. I knew there was something to it when my family used to call me 'Thick Head.' I thought it was an insult at the time. Now I know it was insight."

"Ha ha ha. That's too funny. Sounds like you have a great family."

"Most of them are a fun bunch, but there are those I no longer speak to."

"I know the feeling. My family isn't supportive. They hate the fact that I am gay. I don't want to disappoint them anymore by telling them about me. They already treat me like I'm contagious."

"I know the feeling."

"What did they do?"

"That's a long dark story."

"Understood."

"So, what's your story?"

"I've been shunned by my family because I'm gay. I knew I was gay at a very early age. I never told anybody until I was in high school. When my parents found out about my sexual orientation, they kicked me out of the house. My father said he would never support a faggot son. My mother just screamed at me and slapped me several times across the face. When she said 'get out and never come back,' I left forever. I stayed with of one of my classmate's family. I was able to finish high school. I was rejected by my own family, and I used drugs to feel better about myself. After high school I bounced from house to house living with one temporary lover or another. My drug use became heavier. I ended up getting arrested and going to jail. The first time I served two years. The next four times I served three years each. Since the last time I went to jail I haven't used as many drugs. Although I still shoot up every now and again, I have more important things to worry about. Somewhere along my journey in life I contracted HIV. I'm not sure when because I've not only had unprotected sex most of my life, but also because I shared

more needles using drugs with other people than I can count or remember. The number of sexual

partners I've had over the years also eludes me. Most of my partners were while I was high. And

also, because I'm a prostitute. Since I've been selling myself for money, I've used protection. I

don't like to admit it, but most of my clients are men who have been married for a long time. Too

many of them like to abuse me during or after our encounters. I knows it is part of the job, but I

feel humiliated. Over the years, I've tried to contact my family. They've continued to ignore me.

The second time I went to jail was because my family pressed charges against me for

trespassing. When the police showed up to remove me from my family's property, they found

drugs. That's what landed me in jail. If I wasn't using, I would've just been escorted away from

the property. Twice a week I have to go to a clinic to receive treatment for my HIV. I'm

embarrassed by my choices in life, but I know I have to live with them. My future's uncertain. I

know that my life is coming to an end soon. I haven't been told this, but I know the reality and

the truth of my life. I'm grateful to have met wonderful friends, such as you, over the recent

years. I finally feel loved."

Instant Cloud

Victor and I head to Millennium Park, after we stop at a store for food, to meet up with our neighbors and walk back to our neighborhood. April and Ryle are rambunctious, and they are running around playing tag with each other. They weave in and out of people who are lingering around the fire trying to keep warm. I didn't think that the temperature could get any lower, but today is the coldest day on record. We all finish eating, and we gather around several fire drums we've put together. This has created a larger and warmer fire. Thankfully the wind is not blowing this evening, and we're able to dispel most of the cold with the fire. There is light conversation amongst us, and somehow, we get on the subject of science. I remember when I was in elementary school my teacher showed my class an awesome bit of science. Now I decide to share it with the kids and the rest of the group. I was taught that in below freezing temperatures boiling water will turn into a cloud if it is tossed into the air. I bring a pot of water to a boil and everybody stands around watching as if the pot is going to explode. As I toss the water in the air and a cloud erupts from the pan before their eyes, I am greeted by mixed responses. I was trying to fascinate the kids, and I did. The others in the group seemed disappointed in my experiment. I guess they were expecting something more impressive.

The rest of the night I'm made fun of because of my lame experiment, but it's all in good fun. I fall asleep rather quickly despite the cold. I guess I sleep well because I wake in the morning feeling refreshed. By refreshed I mean that my mind is clear, and I'm able to think without bouts of dizziness. The rest of my body does not agree. My joints are stiff and my muscles ache. I have to thaw the frozen snot hanging from my nose, but I'm in a good mood. I head to my post wondering if anyone will be stopping to put money in my cup on a February day like today.

I arrive at my usual spot, and there are people everywhere. It is almost like the holidays have arrived again. I haven't seen this many people during the day since the summer, and of course Christmas. I watch the people walk by me. Some contribute to my collection and others pass not noticing me. I watch as their accumulated breath rises from their mouths in clouds and comes together as one. Cars drive by, and their exhaust gathers much the same as the expelled breath into a cloud rising above the city. The buildings stand strong, frozen in place by their foundations. Steam rising from the chimneys becomes one with every building. As I see all of this happening, I notice that the sky has clouded over, and the sharpness of the cold air seems to smooth. The temperature rises a bit as the day goes by, and more people join the already crowded sidewalks. My cup is filled with money and emptied into my stash many times throughout the day. My stash grows large, just as the clouds have above me.

Steel Fists

The rest of the week goes by exceptionally well. The temperature has risen above freezing, which is odd for being one week deep in February. Crowds of people swarm the city. Each day my cup overflows with offerings. At one point I have to replace my cup with a new one. All of the excessive use has caused my old cup to fall apart. The weekend arrives, and everyone is in good spirits. I only work for a few hours today. I spend the rest of Saturday with Marissa and the kids. We walk around Millennium Park and the kids play around the bean. Some of the faces the kids make to their own reflections in the bean are distorted into even funnier faces by the shape of the bean. I try a few faces myself. I don't recognize myself. Something about me has changed from when I started this venture.

We head back to our neighborhood and get ready to settle for the night. The kids are full of energy from being able to run around the park, and everybody else is in good spirits due to the warmer weather. There are still fires burning in several oil drums because it isn't warm enough to go without them. Dinner is cooked and passed around amongst all of my friends and neighbors. Marissa and the kids keep to themselves for dinner as usual. Nobody feels this is odd because they respect her for taking care of her children. After we eat and some drink merrily, a few of us head back to our sleeping areas while others stay by the fire and share stories. I look over to Marissa and notice that the children have already fallen asleep. Marissa is bundled up reading a book by Nora Roberts but I can't read the title. I decide to settle in for the night myself. I pull myself into my sleeping bag and pull the covers up over my head. I drift off to sleep, and dream of home and what I have left behind.

Sunday arrives and I wake with a start. I am not sure why my eyes have snapped open so quickly, but soon discover that the pain in my muscles hasn't escaped me during my sleep. Harriet slumbers at my feet. Although my head is healing nicely from the injury, I have a bit of a headache this morning. The world around me spins for a second before I get my bearings. Nobody is in the neighborhood, except for Henry. I'm not quite sure what time it is, but as I look at the sun's position in the sky, I believe it is almost noon. I gather myself and go about my morning routine. Once I finish, I head to my spot on Michigan Ave. Victor is once again sitting near my place, and he is smiling. As I approach him, he chuckles to himself.

"Good morning beautiful. I thought you were going to sleep forever. Nice of you to join the world."

"Good morning to you too. I guess I needed sleep so my body could recover from all of this. Problem is, I feel worse than ever today."

"Life on the street is something you never get used to. Too many times I just want to stay in a hotel room for one night and enjoy a comfortable bed. Unfortunately, I can't afford that. I don't get to see hotels or houses even from my clients. We usually end up in a car or in a back alley behind some building. Nothing is ever easy on the streets."

"I know, I can feel it in my muscles and bones."

The rest of the day goes by smoothly with the company of Victor. My cup is filled several times with offerings, and when the night sky starts to descend upon us, we head back to meet with our group. The walk back to the neighborhood is quiet. The good mood of yesterday seems to have dissipated. When we all arrive at the neighborhood, we find another charity group handing out soup and blankets. They have been around several nights for the past few weeks. The soup is good. I think it's clam chowder, but I haven't noticed any clam in mine. Marissa and the kids aren't in their house, but this isn't unusual when the charities arrive. They usually show up after the soup bearers leave. Once again, I pass up taking a ride to the shelters to spend the night. The temperature is supposed to drop again tonight to dangerous levels. The charity doesn't want to see any of us die. They seem genuinely concerned for us. Other charities that have shown up have a few people who want to help us, and the other people act like they only want to finish their community service and get on with their life.

The rest of the night is rough. The cold air arrives and attacks us with steel fists. The fires roar from the oil drums, and those that huddle around them pass bottles of cheap whiskey. I hunker down in my house. I bring out every available blanket and tighten them around me. I drift off to sleep before I know I'm even tired.

Fear

Monday arrives with a cold dry snow falling from the sky. I am the first person awake this morning, which is a surprise after yesterday's episode. Marissa and the kids are not in their hovel. I am not sure why they didn't make it back home, but fear instantly takes hold of me. I hurry about getting ready for the day, and without eating breakfast I run to the twin's school. No students have arrived yet, but the staff and teachers are slowly trickling in for the day. About an hour goes by, and I finally spot Marissa and the twins. I walk up to them quickly. Marissa sees the worry on my face, but I fake "happy" for the kids.

"Good morning. I thought I would see you two off for the day."

"Hi. See you later."

"Wow, that is a quick greeting and dismissal there Ryle."

"We don't want to be late for school, Craig."

"Alright then, April, you had better get inside."

Marissa escorts the twins inside while I wait on the sidewalk a few doors down from the school. She comes out after a few minutes.

"Is everything alright? You didn't come home last night. That isn't like you."

"I couldn't. I didn't want to…I think Marcus spotted me yesterday and was following us. I couldn't lead him to the neighborhood. He would cause trouble, and I can't have my life destroyed by him anymore. I just have to stay hidden for a few days so he can't follow me. I can't let him know where I am. He can't hurt me or my kids."

"Is there anything I can do? Do you want me to follow you to work to make sure he doesn't approach you? Should we call the cops?"

"No, I can't put anybody else in danger. I can handle this. I have been doing it for a long time. I know how to ditch him if he's following me, and I know how to avoid him. I have a place I can go with the kids so everybody is safe. Thank you for everything, but I have to go to work now."

"Marissa wait. I can help. Don't run away. Let me help you."

Before I know it, Marissa has disappeared around the corner. I wonder if I should follow her at a distance to keep her safe. I start off in the direction she left, but I can't find her once I turn the corner she disappeared around. I search for her, but she's nowhere to be found. I head to my spot as usual, but I can't keep my mind off of the dread I'm feeling. My collection cup is filled many times today, but I barely notice the people who have contributed. It doesn't seem like it has taken long for the night to settle in. I take it upon myself to search the three other neighborhoods I know of, where the homeless gather, for Marissa and the twins. My search is fruitless.

I head back to my neighborhood and head straight for my house. I don't talk to anyone, and the others seem to notice that I need to be alone. Well, everybody but Elijah.

"You alright kid?"

"I'm fine."

"If you're fine then you can call me the King of England. You aren't a very good liar."

"I'll be alright."

"I'm sure it will pass, but you need to talk about it."

"I can't…I mean…it isn't for me to tell."

"It's about Marissa, isn't it?"

"Damn, you're good."

"It ain't rocket science kid."

"What do you know about her?"

"She is hiding. I know she is hiding from a man, but who he is I don't know."

"She thinks she saw him following her yesterday."

"Oh. That can't be good."

"She doesn't want to come back here because she wants to keep us safe. It would also lead him straight to the kids. She can't lose them, and they can't lose her. She is scared…no it's more than that. She is in true fear."

"She'll do what's best for her and the kids. If she wanted our help, she would ask for it."

"I know, but it isn't fair. She shouldn't have to live in fear."

"Life isn't fair. We all have our demons. If we don't face them, they will always haunt us."

"That's why I'm worried, Elijah. She isn't facing her demon. She's running."

"Maybe running is her way of facing it. If not, she'll face it on her own time."

"I guess. I just wish there was something I could do."

"You will learn soon enough that you can only help those who want to be helped."

"That doesn't make it any better."

"I know, but it's the best I can do right now. I ain't got no degree in psychology. I only got street smarts and what I learned in the army."

"It's all good, Elijah. At least you tried."

"This weather needs to figure itself out. First it is cold, then it is warm, and now it is really cold."

"Nice way to change the subject. I know what you mean though. This cold is beyond anything I have ever experienced."

"This time of the year is always rough."

Elijah and I pass the rest of the night along with chit-chat. We share a few hotdogs and some bread. When all the others turn in for their slumber Elijah heads over to Henry to check in on him, and then he heads to bed himself. I sit up trying not to think about Marissa and the kids. Before I know it, the morning has arrived. I haven't slept, and I'm tired.

I go about my morning routine without really trying because my mind is not on the tasks I am undertaking. I go to the kid's school, and I hide in the distance. Marissa never shows. I wait over an hour after the last students go inside to see if she might just be running late. I wait in vain.

I head to my collection post. I see Victor down the street talking to a gentleman in a business suit. They look around suspiciously and then head off together hoping not to be seen. An hour goes by before Victor returns, without his gentleman caller, and before I know it, he is walking off with another client. Business seems to be good for him today. My offering cup is full, and I empty it in my coat pocket. I leave a few coins in the bottom of the tattered coffee cup, and I shake them to attract more attention from passersby. It doesn't take long for my cup to fill again. I find shaking my cup helps to fill it many more times than usual today.

With my mind distracted, I walk back to camp alone. I go straight to my place within this dreary world and hide myself away. Nobody bothers me tonight. I fall asleep quickly.

I wake up, and Wednesday has arrived. I once again go to the school, but to no avail. The day passes by too quickly, and I don't remember anything that has happened. I arrive at the neighborhood, and I am happy to see three smiling faces in the hut next to mine.

"Hello there. Glad to see the three of you again."

"We had to sleep in the basement of the school for two nights. Mom knows a lady who cleans the school, and she made us sleep in the boiler room."

"That sounds like fun."

"It wasn't fun, but it was warm. Mom took us upstairs early, and we took showers two days in a row. I'm clean, Craig, smell my hair."

"I can smell the shampoo from here April. How about you Ryle? Did you have fun?"

"No. I wanted to be here. I…wanted…well I like my HOME here."

Marissa ignores Ryle's comment and shoves a sandwich into his hands. Ryle hesitates at first, but then eats greedily. April nibbles her sandwich and hums to herself as she chews. She seems as happy as ever.

"I'm sorry I shut you out. I don't want you to get hurt. I guess I was paranoid. It must not have been Marcus I saw following me. Must have been some random stranger. I see Marcus in everyone, but this time I took it too far. Can you forgive me?"

"I guess. If that's what you want."

Marissa smiles. We spend the rest of the night chatting about the past two days. After the kids fall asleep Marissa settles in for the night. I return *How to Make Choices You Won't Regret* to Marissa.

"When did you get this?"

"Ryle loaned it to me the other day. He was reading, and I guess he felt I needed a book to read myself. I left your bookmark where it was. I think you have made great decisions thus far."

"Thanks."

I walk back to my house next door and head to bed. I fall asleep and realize somewhat sadly I only have four days left of my adventure.

Marcus

I wake up covered in a thick blanket of snow. The heavy wetness of the snow tries to work its way into my sleeping bag, but I knock it off before it can. Somehow my roof box has blown off and has left me exposed. I go about my morning routine and fix my roof before I leave out for the day. The snow starts to fall again, and the plows can't seem to keep up with it. Cars skid all over the roads, and I see my fair share of fender benders. Pedestrians hurry about trying not to fall. Some carry umbrellas to keep the snow off, but everybody else just moves faster so the snow doesn't collect on them. Quite a few people contribute to me today, but most of them miss my cup. I have to take my gloves off to dig the coins off of the slush covered sidewalk. The snow seems to be falling heavier so I decide to call the day early. I've made enough money today, and I don't want to be greedy since I will be leaving in three days. This hits me harder than I realize. I have gotten so used to living on the streets that I can't imagine going back home. What will I say to the others? How will I tell them I have to leave? What will Marissa and the twins do?

I get back to camp. Elijah and Henry are the only other people here when I arrive. Henry seems out of place today because he smiles at me. That's a first. It doesn't take long for other people to trickle in for the night. I'm happy to see Marissa and the twins arrive. We're all standing around the fire cooking. Knowing this is one of the last nights I will spend with my new friends, I splurged on hamburgers for everybody. I knew the twins would appreciate this since it is their favorite food.

"GIVE ME MY KIDS BACK YOU BITCH!"

Everybody turns to the tall, wiry, dissipated, black man shouting at Marissa.

"Is this where you been hiding? You been avoiding me for far too long woman. I want my kids. You give them to me now, and I won't kill you in front of them."

Marissa stands and hides the twins behind her. Bill, Victor, Elijah, Harvey, and I run over to confront who I assume to be Marcus.

"Get back you mother fuckers or I'll shoot you dead."

We all stop abruptly as Marcus waves a gun at us.

"There is no need for this Marcus. Leave Marissa and the kids alone. They are better off without you. Just leave them alone and go get some help. Nobody needs to get hurt here. If you leave now everything will be better for all of us."

"Who the fuck are you to tell me what to do – you piece of shit white mother fucker? I do what I damn well please. Now get back or I'll put a bullet in your head."

Bill, Elijah, Victor, Harvey, and I have slowly stepped between Marissa and Marcus, but Marcus sees what we are doing and proceeds to counter our actions.

"Marcus, go away! You can't have my children. You need help. You are dangerous, and I will not lose my kids. You will have to kill me before I would ever think of giving them to you."

"Kill you? I can arrange that."

Marcus fires a shot towards Marissa, but thankfully it goes wide and misses everyone. The other people in our neighborhood are running off so they don't get shot or involved in this drama.

"That was just a warning. If I wanted to shoot you I coulda."

"Marcus, go away!"

"Not without my kids you bitch."

"GO AWAY!"

Another shot wizzes past our heads. Marcus is so messed up on drugs that his aim is off yet again. The shot hits a support pillar creating a cloud of dust and shrapnel where the bullet hits.

"I ain't gonna say it again. GIVE ME MY FUCKING KIDS YOU WHORE!"

I haven't noticed until now, but the twins are no longer standing behind Marissa. They have run off, but to where I can't say.

"I SAID GIVE ME MY KIDS...AHHHH...ugh...ahh..."

Marcus collapses, and behind him Henry stands with a bloody knife. Everybody is in shock. We can't move. We are stunned by what we have seen, or rather didn't see. In all of the confusion nobody saw Henry. He quietly walked up and stabbed Marcus in the back without anybody knowing he had moved. Henry drops the knife, goes back to his milk crate and sits down. He laughs really loud. And then every bit of life Henry ever had gently flows out of him. He dies with a smile, sitting on his milk crate.

The others in the neighborhood who took off during all of the drama contacted the police. It isn't long after Henry dies before they arrive in huge numbers. Everybody is detained as soon as they arrive. Cold metal handcuffs on a cold snowy day are not comfortable. Lying face down in cold slush makes everything worse. Nobody says a word until the police ascertain that both Marcus and Henry are dead. They sit all of us up and walk us out of earshot of each other. We are questioned individually as to what happened. They don't seem to believe us for some reason.

"Who was this Marcus guy here for? There aren't any kids, and no Marissa around. I think you are full of it. What really happened?"

"She must have run off before you got here. Look at the pillar and you will see the bullet hole. I'm not lying. She was here. That's her box right over there."

The police investigate Marissa's area and find nothing to identify her. They find nothing useful to the case, and they finally let us out of our handcuffs. Marcus' body is removed from the scene, and then Henry's. The police are gone as fast as they arrived. Even though Marissa and the kids ran off, the police are convinced they have solved the case. Either that or they could care less what happens to the homeless.

Bill, Victor, Elijah, and I huddle around the fire. Harvey goes out for a walk. We don't say anything to each other, but we each know what the others are thinking. We continue to eat the rest of our burgers; our chewing is the loudest sounds that can be heard other than the light traffic above us. As the night gets later, the snow fall becomes heaver. We each silently head over to our respective areas and settle in. A few others have returned to the area, and are getting ready for the night. There is no sign of Marissa and the kids. As I drift off to sleep my thoughts are not of Marissa and the kids, but they are about Henry.

Henry

Friday arrives covered in a thick blanket of snow. Traffic overhead is louder than usual, and there are more sirens screeching by than any other day. Marissa's place is unoccupied. The snow gathered on top of everything lets me know that she did not return last night. I fear that I will never see her again. I know that I am leaving on Sunday, and I want to be able to say goodbye. Elijah is packing up all of his belongings. He finishes and walks up to me.

"I hate to do this to you after everything that happened last night, but there is no need for me to stay here. Henry is dead, and my job is done."

"So where are you going to go?"

"Back to Alabama. I have a house there that I own. I paid my debt to Henry. Now it's time for me to return home."

"Debt to Henry?"

"After I returned from the war, I bought a house. I was well on my way to enjoying the rest of life working, and fishing the bayous of Alabama. I came home from work one day and received a phone call. The voice on the other end of the line said they were contacting me because there had been an accident. My information was all they had for an emergency contact. I quickly packed and closed my house up. I called work and told them I wouldn't be able to come in. I boarded a plane and headed to Chicago.

"When I arrived at the hospital where Henry was admitted, I found out what had happened. Henry had been involved in a car accident. His wife and two daughters were killed. Henry was barely hanging on for his life. I sat with Henry every day for the next three months in the hospital. I then checked him into a rehabilitation nursing center. I came by every day and sat with Henry. Henry was alert most days, but as time passed it seemed that his mind was lost more than not. It was one day when Henry was lucid enough to remember what was going on that he asked me to watch over him and protect him. I owed it to Henry, since he had taken a bullet for me. Henry recovered from his accident, but I noticed Henry wasn't himself. The doctors didn't see it, but Henry's mind seemed to have slipped.

"I had moved into Henry's house to help take care of him per Henry's request. During this time, I would be awakened to Henry screaming. Henry was talking and acting as though he were still at war in Vietnam. On many occasions Henry would mistake me for the enemy. He would try to attack me. On other days Henry would relive the accident that killed his wife and daughters. After a few months of this I was forced to put Henry in the psychiatric ward of the hospital.

"The hospital never kept Henry long. They said there were no facilities that would take him long term. I was going to have to make the best of it. It wasn't long after that that Henry lost his home. With nowhere else to go, I moved Henry to the streets of Chicago. He wouldn't leave the city where his family died. I have taken care of Henry for 25 years. There were a few times when Henry would get hospitalized for a lengthy period of time, and I would fly back home to make sure my house wasn't falling apart. I would then fly back to Chicago and take care of my friend. I was true to my word. I was there for Henry from the beginning. I was there to the end."

At that Elijah gives me a hug. I know I will never see him again.

I set out for my collection spot, and to my surprise Bill and Victor are both sitting there. We chat for a while about the events that went down last night.

"Did you know Elijah left?"

"Figured he would be. He paid his debt to Henry."

"That he did Bill. Did you know about that, Craig?"

"Elijah told me about it. He is a good man."

"He is the best. Not like that piece of garbage that came by last night."

"You said it, Victor. It is a shame that Marissa got messed up with a guy like that."

"That's true, Bill, but most people don't start out showing their bad side. It just sucks that the twins had to witness that. And they are going to grow up without a father."

"He wasn't much of a father."

"Right you are Victor."

The rest of the day goes by in silence.

As Bill, Victor, and I are about to close up shop and head back to our neighborhood Harvey makes an appearance. He is wearing his suit from work, and he looks worried.

"Nice digs Harvey."

"What did you do, rob a bank? Bill did you get a good look at his suit?"

"Hey, Harvey. What's up?"

"I was wondering if you could help me with something tomorrow, Craig."

"Sure, buddy. What is it?"

"I'll tell you later. I kinda have to get back. It's going to be a long night for me."

"OK. You know where to find me."

Home

Bill, Victor, and I walk to the gathering place at Millennium Park to meet the others for our nightly walk back. We arrive at our neighborhood, and it feels empty. Henry isn't sitting in his usual place talking to himself, and Elijah's area is empty. A few people who don't walk with us are scattered around the oil drums, and Marissa is trying to get snow off of their blankets while Ryle and April try to build a new roof out of more boxes. I walk up to my area and set my stuff down. I turn and look over at Marissa.

"I don't have to hide anymore, Craig. I'm free."

Marissa embraces me. I hold her while she sobs the events of last night away. April and Ryle join us. Each hugging one of my legs and crying as well. It takes about fifteen minutes before Marissa pulls herself free.

"Thanks for that. I needed it."

"Anytime. You alright? I didn't think I would ever see you again."

"I'm great. I'm relieved that this is all over. I talked to a girl at work today, and she said there is an apartment for rent near her. I went over there today and talked to the landlord, and she said I can move in immediately. The rent isn't bad, and each of the kids will have their own room. I was wondering if you could help me move in tomorrow."

"Wow. Tomorrow, huh. I'm not sure if I can carry all of these blankets by myself."

"I found some furniture at a second-hand store today. I've been saving all of my paychecks in case one day Marcus was no longer an issue, and we could get off the streets. I used some of it and bought us some nice stuff. My friend from work said she and her husband would pick it up in his truck and deliver it tomorrow. I need help moving it in and setting it up. Are you willing to help?"

"Sure. I can do that, but until then I think we need to eat."

I begin prepping my dinner, and Marissa prepares hers as well. Nobody shares any food tonight. We each cook our food and go back to our areas to eat. I sit on the milk crate Elijah left for me and eat my food. When I finish, I put away my utensils and take as big a swig as possible from my partially frozen water bottle. Harvey approaches me. He is dressed in his street garb, and motions with his head for me to walk with him. I get up and fall into step beside him.

"I found a place to live. I found a home."

"That's great. When are you moving in?"

"Tomorrow. I don't have anything to move in, but I was wondering if you would come with me to sign the lease. I have to have a witness and a reference. I was wondering if you would do that for me."

"Sure thing. What time?"

"I got to meet the guy at 9:00. Is that too early for you?"

"Not at all. Nine it is."

"Thanks, Craig. I really appreciate it. I don't want the others to know so that is why I wanted to take a walk with you. As bad as this sounds, I don't want any bums showing up at my place begging for a place to stay and causing trouble. I know you won't do that to me."

"How do you know I won't do that?"

"I saw your picture the other day. You didn't have a beard, and you were dressed nice, but I know it was you."

"Where did you see my picture?"

"On the back of your book. I know your name isn't Craig either. Your secret is safe with me. I won't tell anybody."

"I'm surprised."

"Why're you surprised that I won't say anything?"

"That isn't what surprises me. I'm surprised you found a copy of my book."

"I even bought it. I started reading it. Great book so far."

Harvey and I walk back to the neighborhood after stopping for coffee. He goes over to his little piece of heaven for what is going to be his last night on the street. I return to my spot and settle down for the night. The twins are wrapped up in their blankets and reading. Marissa is wrinkling up newspaper and stuffing it in her jacket. It has been a few days since I have stuffed myself with new newspaper, so I pick up my collection of papers and fill my jacket.

The morning starts early. I get ready for my day, and then go and get coffee. Harvey meets me at the coffee shop and we head to his new apartment. He managed to find a condo on Lake Michigan through a connection at work. Even though Harvey lost everything he had worked for he managed to have good credit and easily qualified for the condo. Despite his good credit, the leasing company requires a reference. We meet the landlord and fill out the appropriate paperwork. Harvey thanks me, and I headed back to the neighborhood to meet with Marissa.

Marissa has found a cute little three-bedroom apartment off of Roosevelt Rd. We arrive shortly after noon, and her friend is waiting for us. Marissa's friend has no idea that Marissa and the twins have been living on the street. Her friend gives me a once over, but determines that I am harmless. We move the three beds, couch, and table into the apartment. Marissa orders pizza for everybody to thank them for helping. After the pizza is gone Marissa's friend leaves. Marissa, the twins, and I sit at the table.

"Why don't you kids go to your rooms and put away the clothes I got you. The hangers are in the closet."

"Been a fun day."

"I never thought this day would come. Marcus is finally out of our lives, and I'm free to live again. I'm free to live my life without fear. I finally have a place to call home"

"You seem happy. I'm sure the kids will get along fine. Will they be in the same school?"

"They will be until the end of the year. I'll have to transfer them after that since I'm in a new school district."

"I'm glad things are looking up for you."

"It's going to be wonderful. I hope you will stop by every now and then. You don't have to be a stranger."

I hear a crash come from Ryle's room.

"It was an accident mom. I'm OK."

Marissa heads to Ryle's room with a broom and dustpan. I take this opportunity to slip out the door unnoticed. Before I go, I pull my earnings for the month out of my pocket. I know it isn't much, but the few thousand dollars I earned during my month on the street should serve Marissa and the twins well. Without them knowing, I slip out the door and quietly say goodbye.

I head back to the invisible neighborhood under the freeway and sit on my milk crate. Bill winks at me when I look over in his direction, and Victor gives a quick wave. I gather all of the belongings that I am taking with me tomorrow in my backpack. I cook myself one last meal and then join the others at the oil drum. I don't say anything, but I laugh at the appropriate times. The night is solemn. I am missing the few who are no longer living with us – Elijah, Henry, Eric, Harvey, and Marissa and the Twins. The night continues, and I head to bed.

Morning arrives, and I wake to the cold air greeting me. Everybody is heading out for the day, and I take my time getting ready. I make sure everybody is gone before I fold up my blankets, sleeping bag, and pillow. I leave them in a nice pile under my cardboard mansion. I find a piece of paper and a pen. I write "Goodbye" across the paper and tuck it in a fold of the sleeping bag so it won't blow away and the others will see it. Harriet curls up on top of the sleeping bag. I give her a quick scratch before I head off. I am sad as I leave from my adventure. I know that too many people I have encountered during my journey will never advance out of their homeless situation. Too many will die propped up against a wall begging for change or lying on makeshift beds of worn blankets and cardboard. I start walking to Ogilvie Station. Along the way the homeless are no longer invisible to me. I see people wearing tattered clothing and begging for change everywhere. Why have I never noticed them before? There are so many. One man sitting on a wall on Adams between Michigan and Wabash singing random words to a song that makes no sense. A group of men play their five gallon-bucket-drums whose resonating beat echo off of the towing skyscrapers just down from Union station. I board a train, and I travel to my destination. My prearranged ride is waiting for me to take me home.

I enter my front door. My home is alien to me. After a month of being exposed to sometimes below freezing temperatures, the warmth of the furnace is overwhelming. I head to my bathroom and take off the clothes I have been wearing for a month. Crumpled newspaper falls to the floor. My filthy clothes lay in a pile next to the trash can. I look in the mirror. I don't recognize the person staring back at me. I have lost at least twenty pounds. My face is covered in a thick beard. My eyes look hollow. I am no longer myself.

A Month in the Making

I set out to live on the streets of Chicago for thirty days. I was tired of writing fictional stories, and wanted to write the truth. The experience I lived, as described in this story, was not what I had expected. I found a story to write, but I also lived it. I learned not only my own vulnerability, but the vulnerability of every person on this planet. I found that everybody is only one mistake, the loss of one job, or one decision away from living on the street. This realization has brought me to care less for material possessions, and more for the people that surround me.

Since my experience, I have volunteered with many organizations to help those in need. I help veterans who have experienced traumatic events in war and other aspects of their life to transition back into civilian life. When I looked at myself in the mirror the day I returned home, I did not recognize myself. It wasn't because I was dirty, unshaven, and had lost weight. It was because I had changed. During my experience I had lost myself, and on my return, I found who I am supposed to be. I am a person I never knew or expected to be. My experience brought forth a revelation. I am no longer greedy or selfish. I live off of very little and give the rest to those who need it. I have found the true me.

Made in the USA
Middletown, DE
08 April 2022

63866943R10050